Introduction

Easy to Make! Easy to Read!

Young children get excited reading about things that relate to their everyday experiences. But they get even more excited when they can help create the art and text in these reading materials. The books in the *Make Your Own Emergent Readers* series provide children with interactive, personalized reading experiences by inviting them to investigate, complete sentence frames, illustrate, put together, and create covers for their very own readers. Each book in the series contains 10 eight-page themed reproducible books for emergent readers. These easy-to-read Little Books contain text that is simple, predictable, and repetitive, and usually have one or two new words or changes on each page. The books present various subject matter following a specific theme.

This resource, *Around the Community*, provides everything you need to get children excited about reading as they create their very own library of self-made and illustrated books about their community.

Creative Suggestions and Activities

Pages 3–7 provide creative suggestions and activities for each Little Book, including:

Cover Idea—Tells you how to create a colorful, eye-catching cover using a variety of art techniques and mediums.

Ideas for Illustrating Inside Pages—Help you guide children to add their own text to many of the books and creatively illustrate the pages.

Extension Activities—Provide unique ways to extend learning concepts presented in the Little Books as well as encourage further reading and writing.

Literature List

A comprehensive list of related books is provided on page 8. Use these books as read-alouds, research material, and extra books children can read on their own. Theme-related read-alouds enhance your literacy program by providing background knowledge and extending the concepts introduced in the content areas.

Directions for Making the Little Books

Putting the Pages Together

Reproduce the pages for each Little Book. *Do not cut pages in half!* Children can fold the pages and place them in numerical order. The pages will be doubled, and text will read on both sides. This unique page construction creates more durable books for frequent rereading. Also, creating artwork is easier. Markers and paint will not bleed through, and the pages are more suitable for collage materials.

Note: Depending on the art technique used, it may be easier for children to illustrate each page before assembling books, especially if it's a messy technique! Have extra pages available for "mess-ups." Once the art is complete and pages are in order, fold the pages on the dotted line and bind them together. Stapling is the easiest, but pages can also be hole-punched and bound with ribbon or yarn.

© Frank Schaffer Publications, Inc.   FS-69007 Around the Community

Adding a Cover and Completing the Pages

- The first page of each Little Book can serve as the cover. However, you may choose to follow the cover suggestions on pages 3–7, or invite children to each make a special, individualized cover of his or her own. Make two covers at a time by cutting 12" x 18" (30 cm x 45 cm) construction paper in half lengthwise, and then folding each piece in half.
- The inside pages can be illustrated quickly and easily by drawing and/or coloring. (Refer to the Literature List on page 8 for books that help children learn to draw.) Peruse pages 3–7 for directions (in many instances, children are asked to complete existing art and/or draw inside borders or frames) and suggestions for implementing creative, visually-exciting art techniques. These suggestions are a great way to integrate the arts into your program, and children will love experimenting with collage materials, pastels, paint, crayon-resist, cut paper, and more!
- In advance, make several photocopies of your class picture. Children can use their own pictures whenever a self-portrait or photo is called for in the art. Or, you can use photocopied pictures to create a "Meet the Author" page for special books.
- You may also attach a "comments" page on the inside back covers of the books. Here children can dictate or write their feelings about the book, what they learned, or more text additions to continue the story.
- To encourage rereading, attach a page to the inside back covers on which children can list the people to whom they have read their books.

Using the Little Books

Before children make and read Little Books on their own, introduce them to the text during shared reading activities. Depending on children's reading-skill development, they should have several opportunities to interact with the text before making each Little Book. You can do this in a variety of ways:

- Make a class big book using the text from the Little Book combined with student illustrations. Read the big book several times during shared reading time.
- Make a pocket chart of the Little Book's text, along with matching picture cards.
- Make overhead transparencies of the Little Book's text and art.

Just think of how proud children will be showing off their own creatively-designed books to their classmates and families!

There are a myriad of ways to use these books in your classroom and at home, but here are just a few suggestions on how to incorporate the Little Books into your literacy program:

- Learning-center activities
- Extra reading in the content areas
- As an introduction to various subjects
- Independent reading material
- Homework activities
- Reading material for the child at home
- Practice with sight words

Creative Suggestions and Activities

Let's Walk

Cover Idea
Paint a colorful map showing the route of the walk through your immediate neighborhood. Add collage materials and cut paper to add details such as homes and trees.

Inside Pages
Create a list of stores, landmarks, and other places found in a community. Refer to the list to finish the text on pages 5–7. Add an extra page to the Little Book, so you can write about and illustrate a fun place in your community that you like to visit, such as the park, candy store, or library.

Extension Activities
- Take a walk around the school grounds. Take notes on the things you pass on your walk. Use your notes to help children create a class book. For example: *We walked past the flagpole. But we didn't walk past the library. We went in to hear a story.*
- Have fun with music and movement! Choose "sign posts" in your room, such as your desk, the front door, and the flag. Have children walk around the classroom to music and chant, *Let's walk past the teacher's desk, let's walk past the door, and let's walk past the flag.* Stop the music and have a child choose a new verb (e.g., *dance*). Now chant, *Let's dance past the teacher's desk, let's dance past the door, and let's dance past the flag.* Keep stopping the music and choosing new verbs such as *skip, hop, fly,* and *swim.*

Where _____ Lives

Cover Idea
Decorate a lightweight tagboard paper doll as a self-portrait. Attach the doll to the cover with yarn or ribbon, and store it in a house-shaped pocket attached to the front.

Inside Pages
Finish the text and art on each page to tell about where you live, starting from your home and ending with the planet we all share. On page 6, color in or outline the state in which you live. When reading your finished book, place your paper doll self-portrait on each page.

Extension Activities
- Send blank copies of the Little Books to several children who live in other states and/or communities. Perhaps children in the class could recommend cousins or other relatives. Ask each pen pal to finish writing and illustrating the pages and send the books back to your class. Invite children to compare and contrast the information in these Little Books with their own.
- Cut a large triangle from butcher paper. Make a class chant, starting at the top: *We learn in a school on (street's name). We learn in a school in (city or town's name). We learn in a school in (state's name). We learn in a school in (country's name). We learn in a school on (continent's name). We learn in a school on planet Earth!* The triangle will help children see the progression from their small community to the world at large. Make another triangle chant, but place the triangle upside down, starting with planet Earth.

Where Do People Live?

Cover Idea
Fold a 12" x 18" (30 cm x 45 cm) piece of construction paper in half, then "double-cut" a simple shape representing the building in which you live. Then decorate the cover to look like your real home using collage materials. Staple the Little Book inside the cover.

Inside Pages
Color the pages using brightly-colored crayons or markers. Draw a self-portrait on page 7, and then write about and illustrate the community where you live on page 8.

Extension Activities
- Make a big book titled *If I Could Live Anywhere!* Have children write where they would like to live and why, and illustrate their writing on butcher paper. Decorate the cover of the book with cutouts from travel brochures and magazines.

- Ask student groups to paint a mural of one of the different communities where people live. Then have them write the advantages and disadvantages of life in that community to add to their murals.

Maps of My Favorite Places

Cover Idea
Ask parents to donate outdated maps to your class recycling box. Use pieces of old maps to make a collage for the cover.

Inside Pages
Before children complete the Little Books, help them with "mapping" skills by drawing a map of your classroom on the chalkboard. Then make a set of "mapping" directions for children to follow as they color the art on each page. For example, *Add a rug east of the bed on page 2.*

Extension Activities
- As an introduction to map-making, arrange various school items on your desk, and make a map of your desk. Make sure to include a key for the map. Have each child examine the map and your desk to get a "feel" for how maps work. Then invite them to follow the format of the Little Book to make their own map books about their favorite places. Two wonderful books to use as resources are *Me on the Map* by Joan Sweeney and *My Map Book* by Sara Fanelli.

- Go on a treasure hunt! Have each child choose a partner. Each child brings in or makes something special for his or her partner (e.g., candy, marbles, a special letter). He or she then decides where to hide the treasure, and makes a map from his or her partner's desk to the where the treasure is hidden. Children then hide their treasures, trade maps, and go on a treasure hunt!

© Frank Schaffer Publications, Inc.   FS-69007 Around the Community

Helping Hands

Cover Idea
On a black or dark blue cover, make several brightly-colored tempera paint handprints. Each child can dip his or her hand in different-colored paint and make prints on each other's covers.

Inside Pages
Brainstorm a list of community helpers and discuss the services they perform. Use the list to complete the text on each page. Then draw each community helper described in the text.

Extension Activities
- Ask children to interview a family member about his or her job. Have them present short oral reports of the information they learned. List the various jobs of children's family members, and marvel at the way each person contributes to the community.
- Read *Jobs People Do* by Christopher Maynard. A child appears on each page dressed as the featured worker. Imitate the book's format by inviting each child to research the job of one worker. He or she can wear a simple costume while telling the class about the worker's job.

Community ABC

Cover Idea
Decorate the cover with cutouts and drawings of objects you see in your community every day (e.g., stop sign, crossing guard, schoolhouse). Use letter sponges and colorful tempera to complete the title, printing *ABC* across the cover.

Inside Pages
Brainstorm other community "places" and people to add to the Little Book. For example, *Aa–airport, Bb–baseball field, Cc–car wash*. You may add extra pages or more words to each existing page. Look through your local phone book to help find places that supply goods and services in your community.

Extension Activities
- Discuss the difference between "needs" and "wants." Divide a sheet of butcher paper into two columns and label columns *Who Supplies Our Needs?* and *Who Supplies Our Wants?* Make word cards by cutting apart an extra copy of the Little Book. Place each "card" in the appropriate column. If a word seems to fit both categories, place it on the line between the two columns. Or, attach the word cards to a Venn diagram.
- Make a big book modeled after the Little Book. Give each child a letter of the alphabet and a 12" x 18" (30 cm x 45 cm) piece of construction paper. Have him or her illustrate a page, and either copy the text of the Little Book or come up with his or her own words, adding *where I _____*. For example, *Aa is for Animal Shelter, where I pet the kitties; Nn is for Nursery, where I buy my rose bushes.*

Community Cleanup

Cover Idea

Draw, color, and cut out a picture of yourself and glue it to the cover. Then, cut a miniature trash bag from a real trash bag and glue it to your portrait's hand. Draw a park scene in the background and "litter" it by gluing on scraps of paper, tin foil, and so on.

Inside Pages

Color or paint the illustrations on each page. Then add various "collage materials" for texture. For example, add "trash" scraps to page 2; small, dry leaves to page 3; yarn to the mop on page 4; bright-colored tissue paper to the flowers on page 6; and green paper scraps or tissue to the tree on page 7. On page 8, draw yourself playing with a friend in the cleaned-up park.

Extension Activities

- Have a Cleanup Day at school each week! During part of recess on that day, you and your class can donate your time to campus cleanup. You may also want to "adopt" a small area on school grounds that is looking scraggly, and plan a way to spruce it up (plant flowers, shrubs, grass, or a small garden).

- Introduce the idea that families are part of the community. Tell children that they can help the community by helping their own families. As a class, brainstorm ways children can help at home. As homework, have children present "How Can I Help?" tickets to parents or other family members. After a job at home is completed, parents can sign the ticket and send it back. Invite children to share with the class how they helped at home.

City People

Cover Idea

Create a cityscape on a black cover. Cut skyscrapers and other city buildings from newspaper to glue on the cover. Use black crayon or marker to outline the buildings and add details such as windows, doors, and signs.

Inside Pages

Outline parts of the background art with black crayon. Use watercolors to paint within the lines. Color in remaining art with colored pencils or markers. Cut faces of people from magazines and glue them to people on the pages.

Extension Activities

- Share the book *Rush Hour* by Christine Loomis. Make a class version of the Little Book, expanding the text to include people in your community. For example:
  People walking.
  People walk to the bus stop.
  People walk to Schenley Park.

- Read the fable *The City Mouse and the Country Mouse*. Invite children to rewrite the Little Book as *Country People*, and illustrate farmland, vast blue sky and open spaces, people working the land, and so on.

© Frank Schaffer Publications, Inc.

FS-69007 Around the Community

Guess Who's in Your Community

Cover Idea
Decorate the cover with a collection of hats or objects associated with community helpers. You can include hats of a firefighter and policeman, along with items such as a stethoscope, book, and tooth.

Inside Pages
Complete the text on each page, color the backgrounds, and draw the appropriate community helper: *checker, veterinarian, police officer, paramedic, letter carrier,* and *librarian.* On page 8, draw yourself in your neighborhood. When the text and art are complete, add a "lift-and-look" flap over each helper's name, so the reader can guess the answer.

Extension Activities
- Invite a community helper to the class to speak about his or her job. Afterwards, make a large cutout of the person from butcher paper. Invite children to paint and decorate the cutout to resemble your guest. Then write about your guest and his or her job on the shape and display it in the classroom. Take a picture of the cutout and mail it to your guest speaker with a class thank-you card.
- Make the Little Book into a riddle game! Divide the class into two teams. Pose riddles from the Little Book for children to answer. Make sure to call on every child. Keep points for correct answers. Invite children to make more riddles using other occupations such as garbage collector, bank teller, custodian, construction worker, nurse, window washer, and so on.

_____'s Week

Cover Idea
Create a border on the cover by writing the days of the week in large letters around the edges. Write them in pencil first and then trace over the letters with colored glue. Add a cutout of yourself, from the shoulders up, and decorate it with collage materials.

Inside Pages
Discuss how our needs and wants are met through resources available in the community. Then finish the text and illustrate each page to show how you use these community resources.

Extension Activities
- Ask children to keep track of where in the community they go during a designated week. Then, using this information, make a class graph that shows how many children used various community services during that week. This helps children realize how dependent they are on their community, and how we all help each other.
- Have children make innovations of the Little Book using months of the year. For example, *In January, I _____.* Brainstorm with children the things that happen during different months, and record them in an "Idea Bank" children can refer to when writing.

Literature List

Ask Me What My Mother Does by Katherine Leiner (Watts)
At the Beach by Ann Rockwell (Simon & Schuster)
The Best Town in the World by Byrd Baylor (Scribners)
The Big Orange Splot by Daniel M. Pinkwater (Scholastic)
Building a House by Byron Barton (Hampton-Brown)
A Busy Day at Mr. Kang's Grocery Store by Alice K. Flanagan (Children's Press)
Check It Out! The Book About Libraries by Gail Gibbons (Harcourt Brace)
City Street by Douglas Florian (Greenwillow)
Everybody Bakes Bread by Norah Dooley (Carolrhoda)
Firehouse by Katherine K. Winkelman (Walker & Co.)
Fireman Jim by Roger Bester (Crown)
Handy Hank Will Fix It by Anne Rockwell (Holt)
How a House Is Built by Gail Gibbons (Holiday)
I Like the Library by Anne Rockwell (Dutton)
I Walk and Read by Tana Hoban (Greenwillow)
Jobs People Do by Christopher Maynard (Dorling Kindersley)
Kimako's Story by Kay Burford (Houghton Mifflin)
The Little House by Virginia Lee Burton (Houghton Mifflin)
Market! by Ted Lewin (Lothrop)
Me on the Map by Joan Sweeney (Crown)
Mr. Grigg's Work by Cynthia Rylant (Orchard)
My Backyard by Ann Rockwell (Macmillan)
My Map Book by Sara Fanelli (HarperCollins)
My Mommy Makes Money by Joyce Mitchell (Little, Brown)
My Street's a Morning Cool Street by Ianthe Thomas (HarperCollins)
Night Story by Ethel and Leonard Kessler (Macmillan)
No Star Nights by Anna Egan Smucker (Knopf)
Once Around the Block by Kevin Henkes (Greenwillow)
Our Neighborhood Series (Children's Press)
People by Peter Spier (Doubleday)
People Working by Douglas Florian (Crowell)
Playgrounds by Gail Gibbons (Holiday)
Police Patrol by Katherine K. Winkelman (Walker & Co.)
Rush Hour by Christine Loomis (Houghton Mifflin)
Secret Places by Beverly Brodsky (Harper)
Smoky Night by Eve Bunting (Harcourt Brace)
Tar Beach by Arthur Getz (Dial)
Toby in the Country, Toby in the City by Frank Modell (Greenwillow)
Up Goes the Skyscraper! by Gail Gibbons (Simon & Schuster)
Whose Hat? by Margaret Miller (Greenwillow)

Drawing Books

Draw Fifty Series by Lee J. Ames (Doubleday)
Ed Emberley's Drawing Book: Make a World by Ed Emberley (Little, Brown)
Ed Emberley's Drawing Book of Faces by Ed Emberley (Little, Brown)
Ed Emberley's Great Thumbprint Drawing Book by Ed Emberley (Little, Brown)
Ed Emberley's Picture Pie: A Book of Circle Art by Ed Emberley (Little, Brown)
I Can Draw Series by Lisa Bonforte (Simon & Schuster)

1

Helping Hands

2 A _____ helps put out fires.

A _____ helps me care for my teeth.

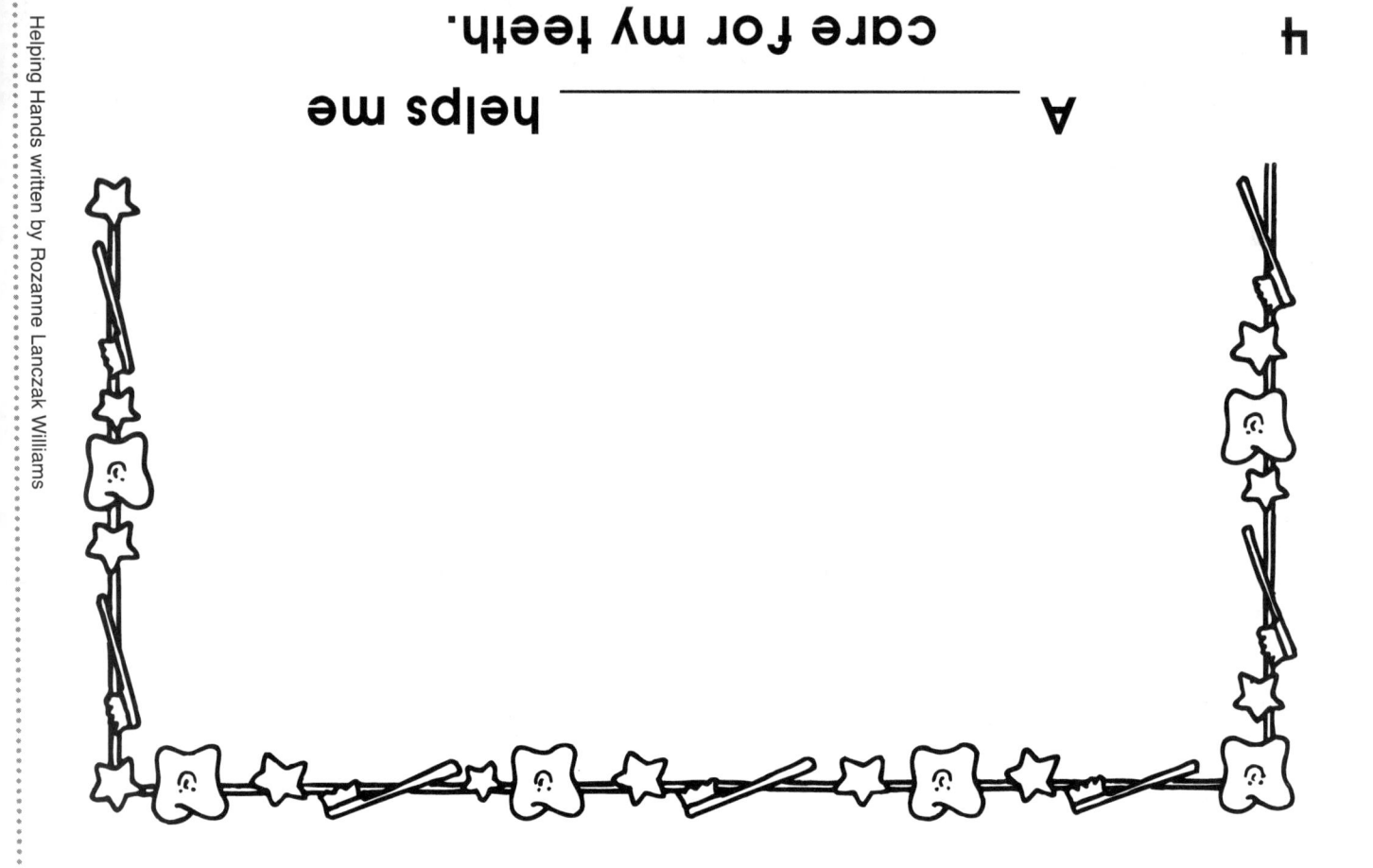

4

A _____ helps me stay healthy.

3

A _____ helps me read the book!

A _____ helps me find a good book.

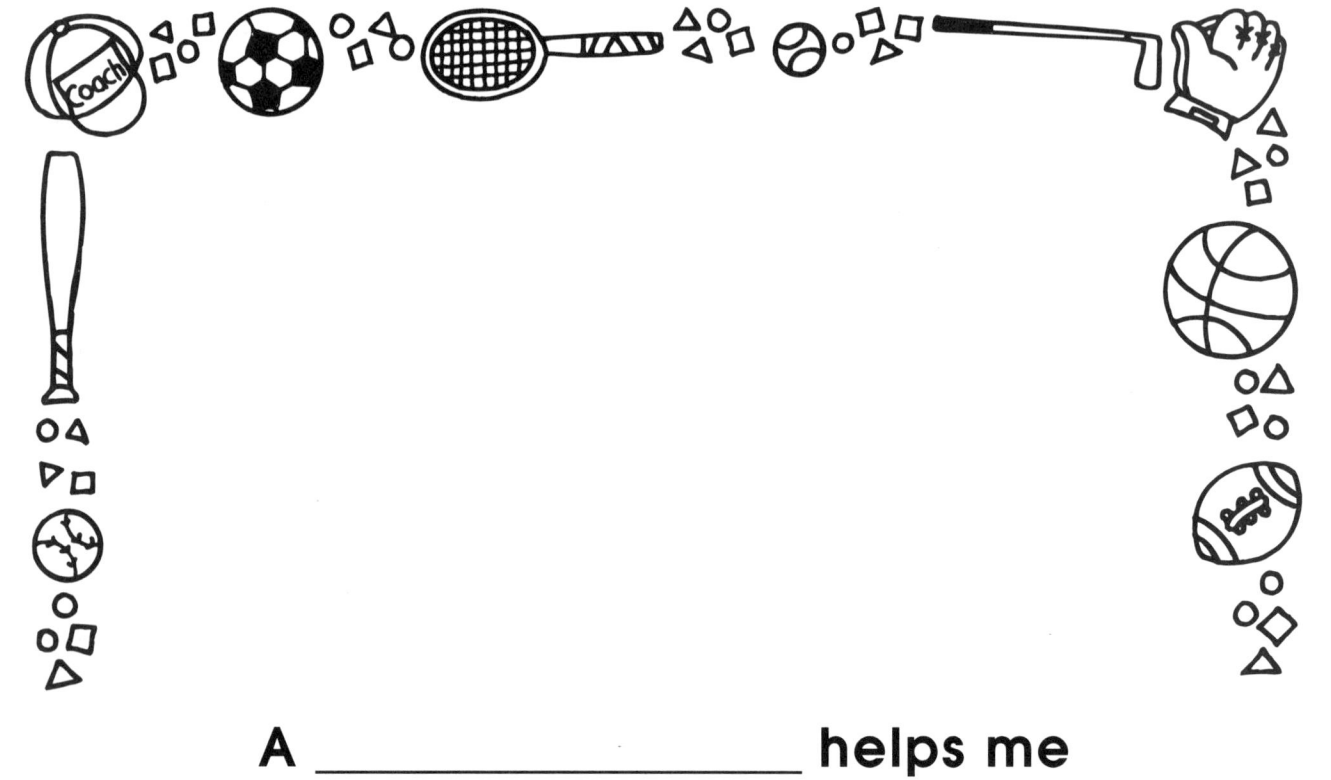

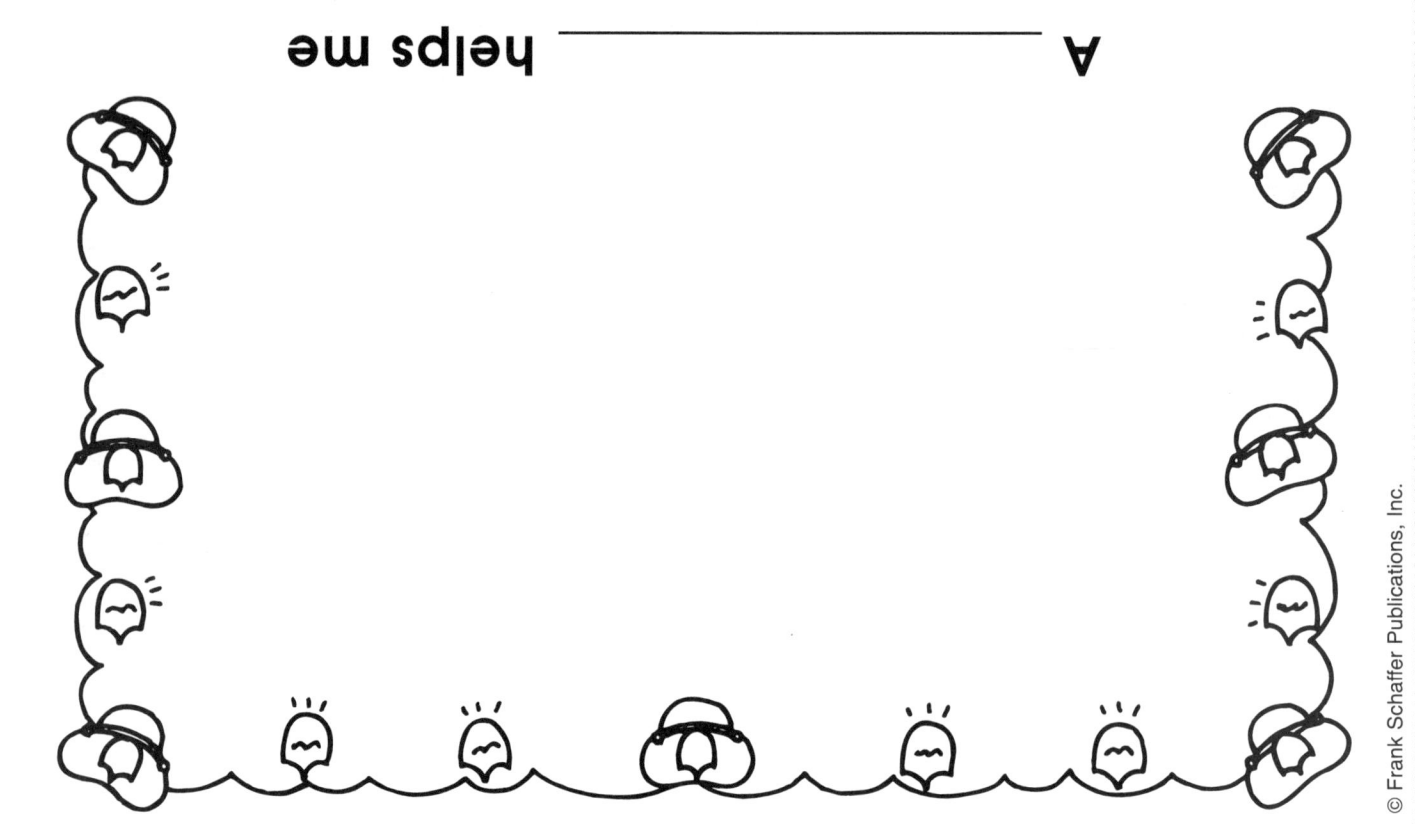

A _____ helps me when I'm lost.

5

A _____ helps me play softball.

6

2 Some people live in the country.

Where Do People Live?

Where do you live?

7

8 I live_____ .

2

Here is a map of my bedroom.

Maps of My Favorite Places

Maps of My Favorite Places written by Rozanne Lanczak Williams

© Frank Schaffer Publications, Inc.

Here is a map of my house.

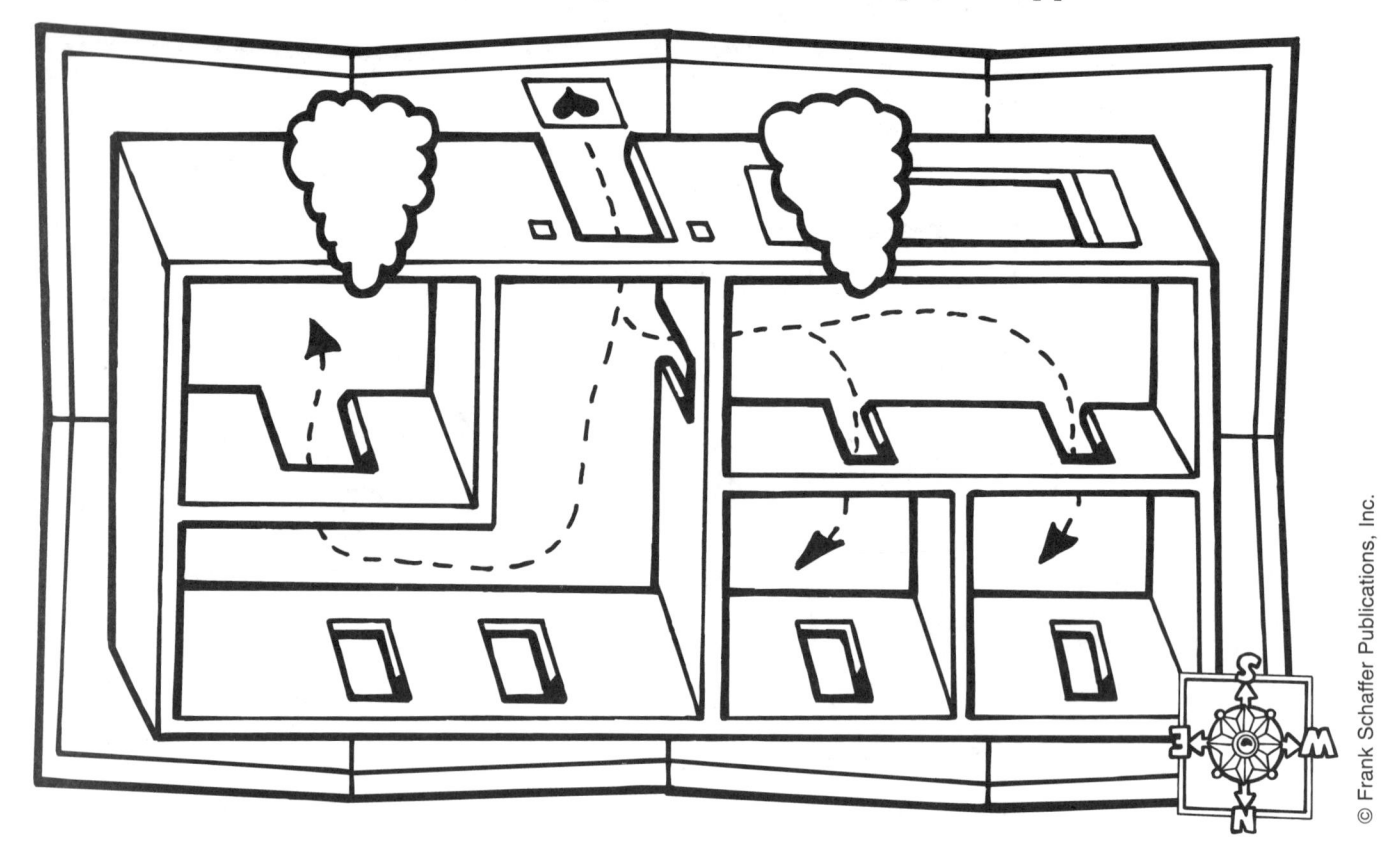

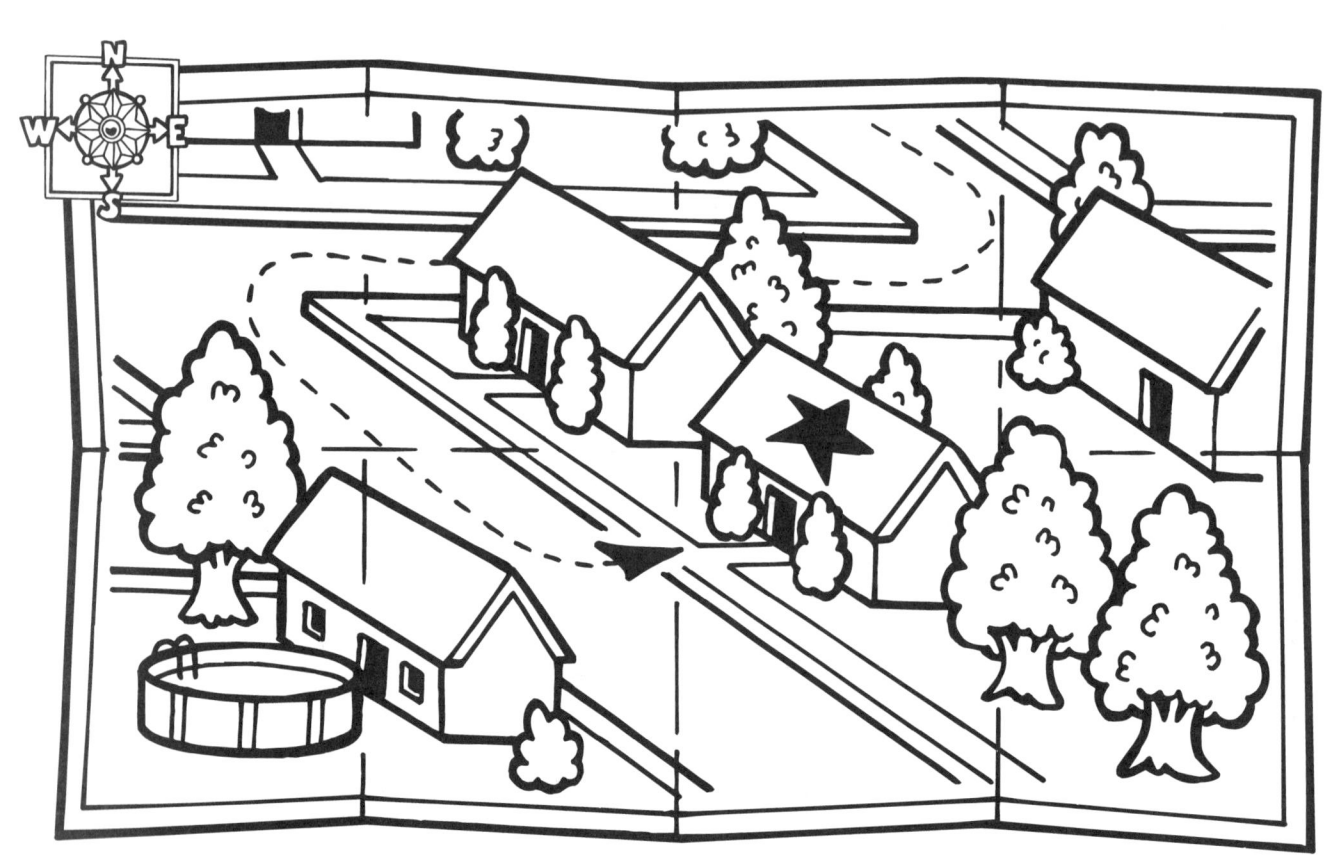

3

Here is a map of my street.

4

Here is a map of my school.

9

Here is a map of the park.

5

Here is a map of my classroom.

7

Here is a map of my neighborhood.
Can you find my favorite places?

8

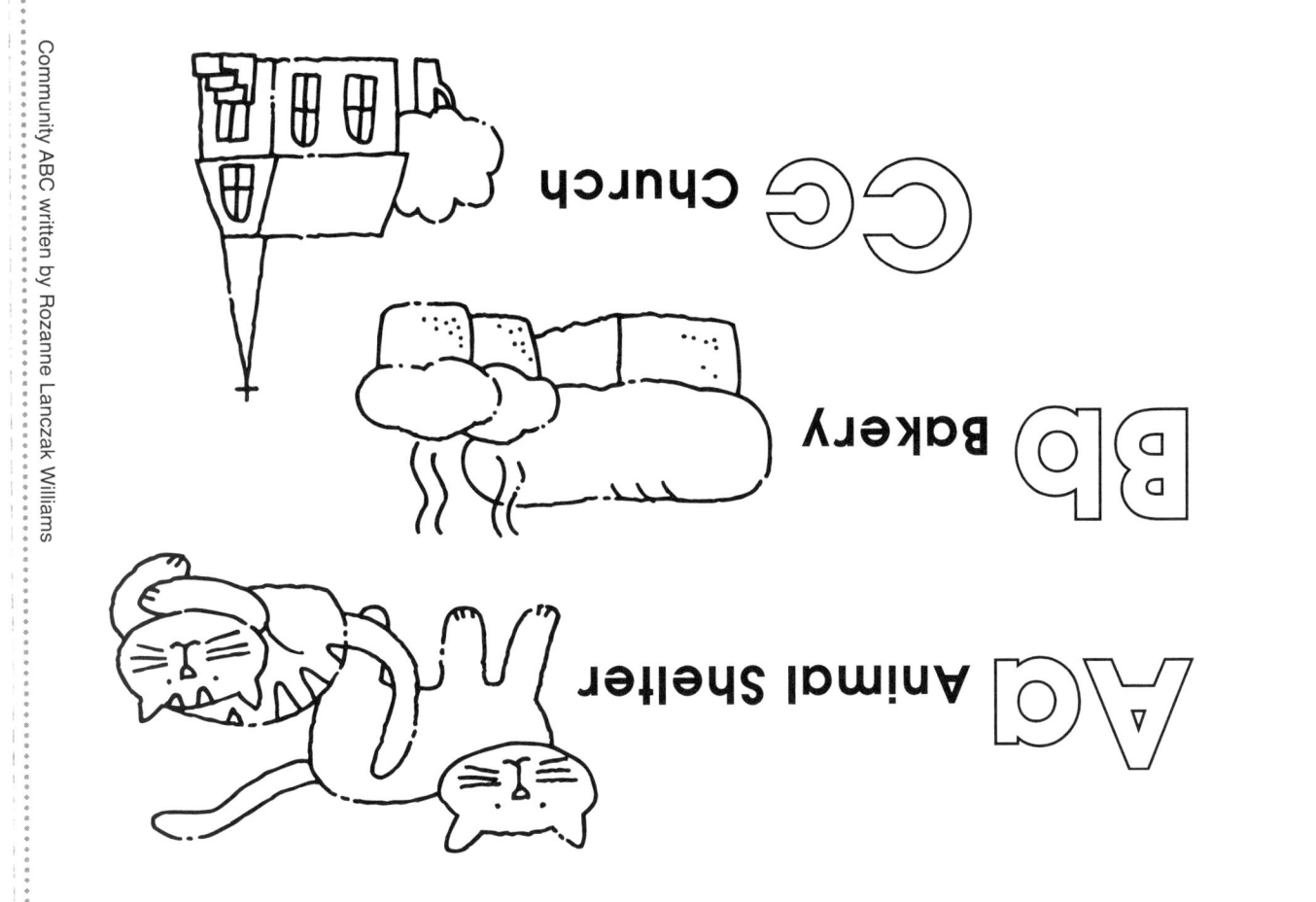

Community ABC written by Rozanne Lanczak Williams

Community ABC

Aa Animal Shelter

Bb Bakery

Cc Church

© Frank Schaffer Publications, Inc.

Dd Doctor's Office

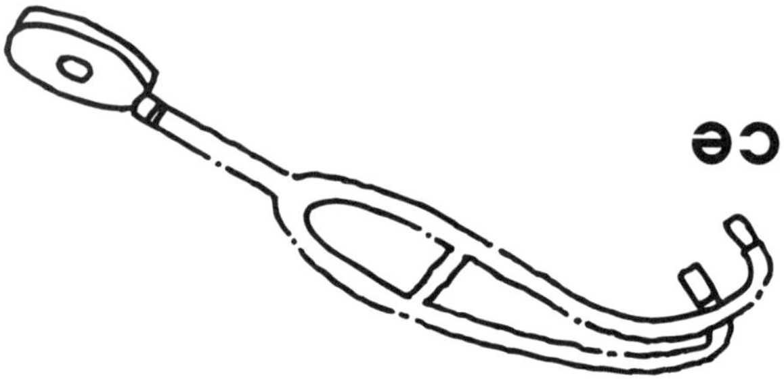

Ee Electric Company

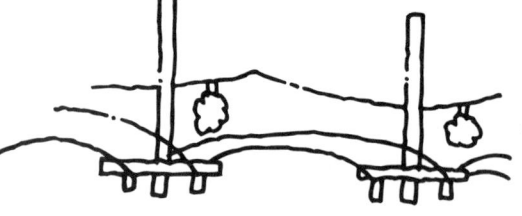

Ff Florist

Gg Gas Station

Hh Hospital

Ii Ice-Cream Parlor

Jj Jewelry Store

Oo Optical Store

Pp Post Office

Qq Quick-Stop Mini Mart

Rr Restaurant

Kk Key Shop

Ll Library

Mm Movie Theater

Nn Nursery

Ss School

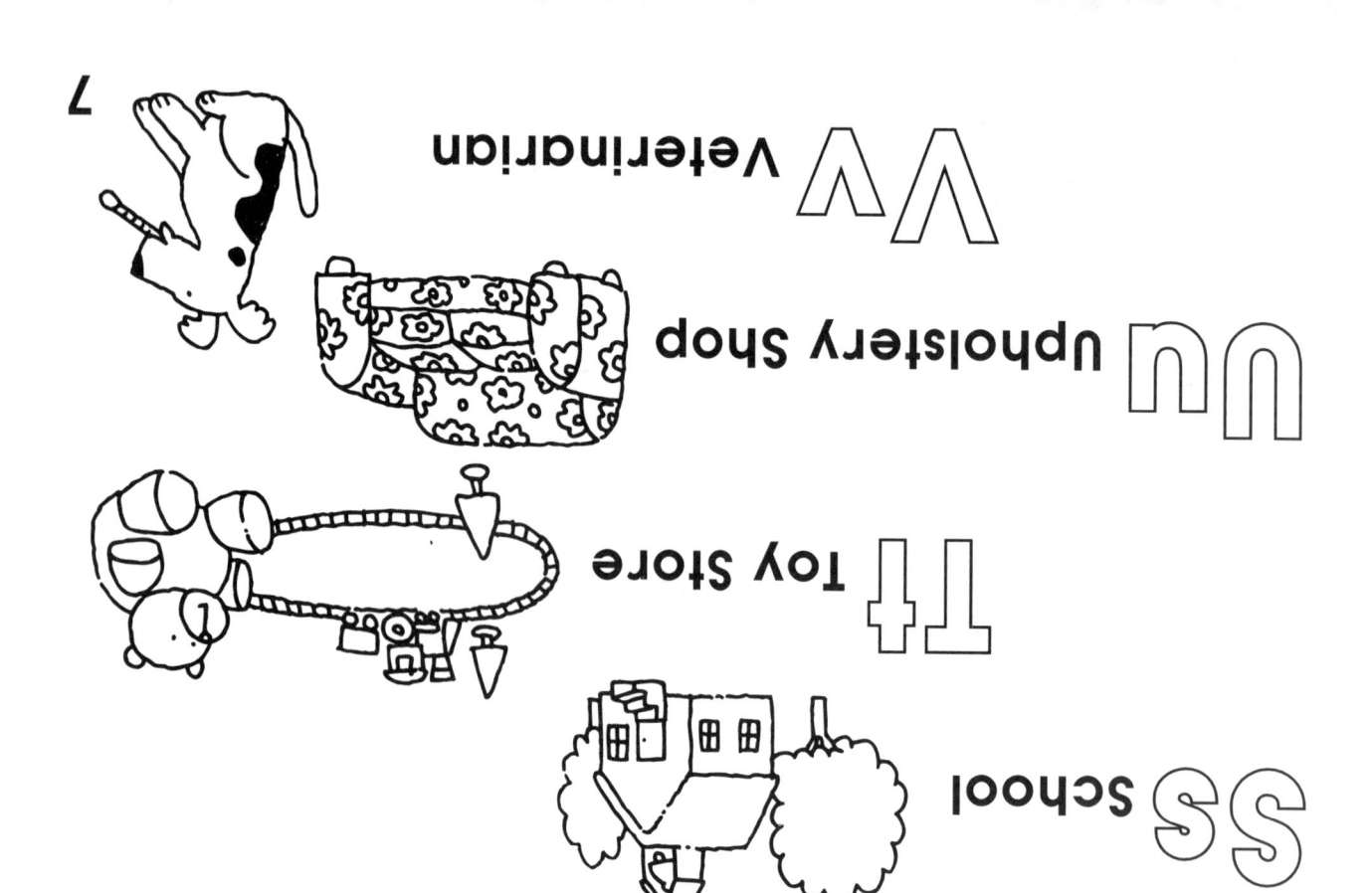

Tt Toy Store

Uu Upholstery Shop

Vv Veterinarian

Ww Weather Station

Xx X-ray Laboratory

Yy Yogurt Shop

Zz Zoo

Let's clean up the park.

2

Community Cleanup

1

Let's clean up the street.

3

Let's clean up the places

4

6

Let's plant some flowers.

5

where we like to meet.

Let's plant a tree.

7

Let's take care of our neighborhood, you, and me!

8

2

People walking.

People talking.

3

People going here and there.

4

People playing.

6

People working.

5

People, people,

7

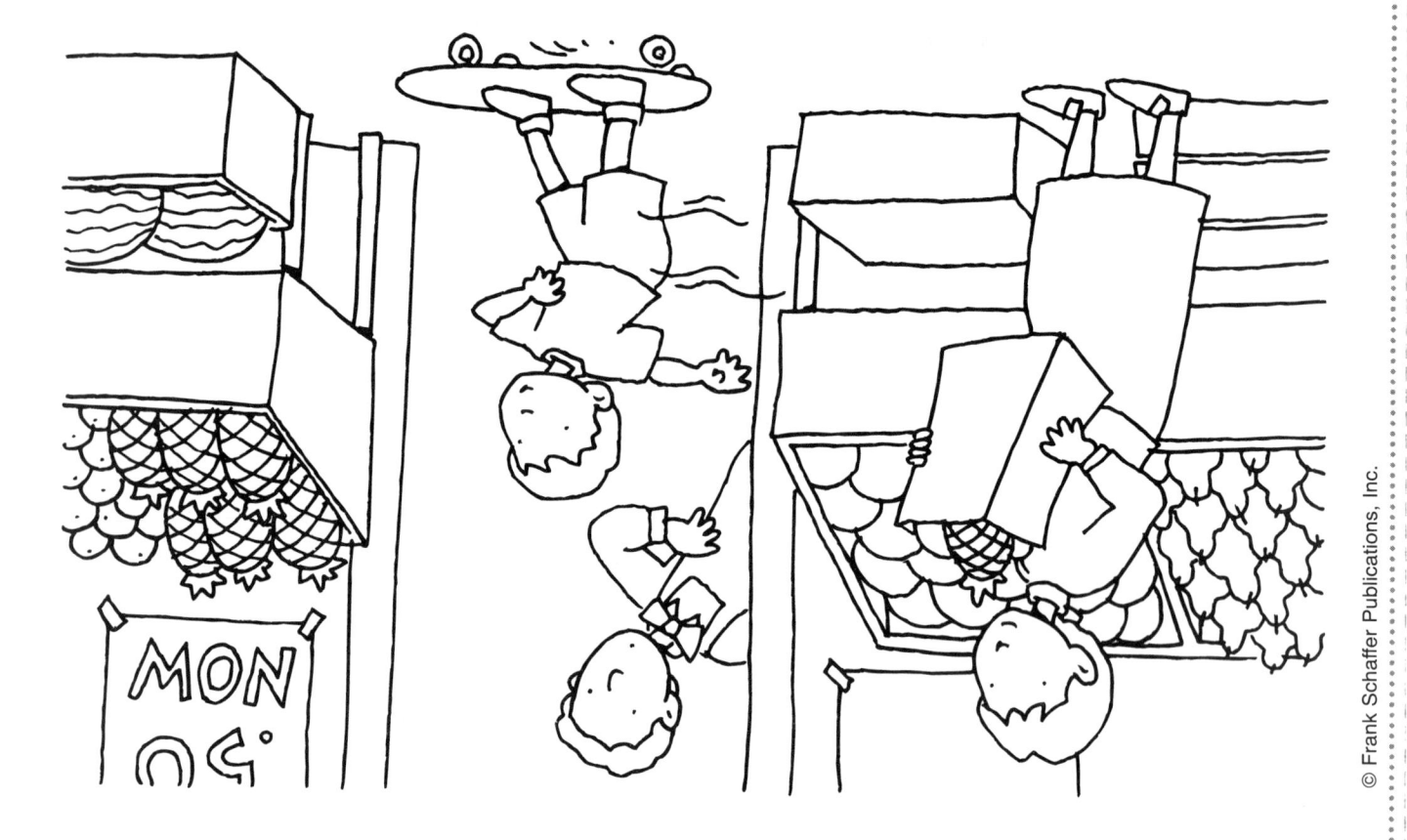

everywhere!

8

2 I am a _____.

I help you at the supermarket.
I work at the cash register.

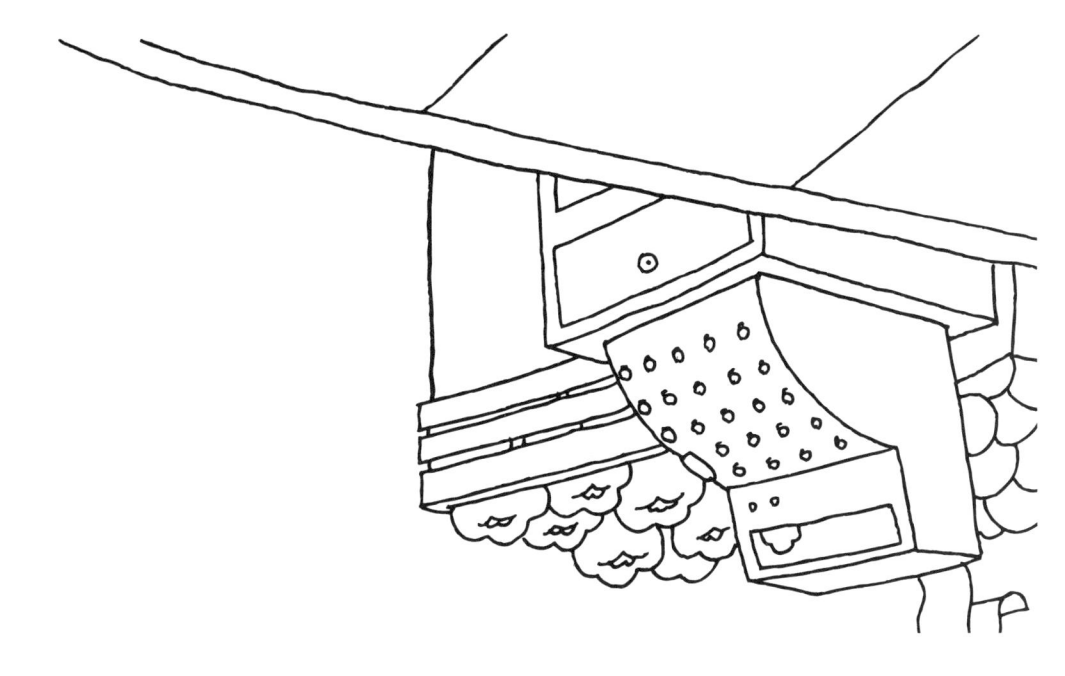

Guess Who's in Your Community

1

I love animals.
I help them when they are sick.
I am a _____.
3

I help keep your neighborhood safe.
I wear a uniform and drive a special car.
4   I am a _____.

6

I am a _____.

Sometimes I bring you a surprise.

I come to your house six days a week.

I help people in an emergency.
I can get to you very quickly.
I am a _____.

5

I work in a library.
I can help you find a good book.
I am a _____.

I am like you and your neighbors.
I help take care of the neighborhood.
I am a good citizen!

_____'s Week

On Monday, I start my week at school.
I learn _____.

On Tuesday, I go to the market.
I buy _____.

3

On Wednesday, I go to the library.
I like books about _____.

4

On Friday, I go to dinner at a restaurant.
I eat _____.

6

On Thursday, I go to the post office.
I mail _____.

5

On Saturday, I go shopping at the mall.
I buy _____.

7

On Sunday, I _____.
I _____.

8